My Uncles and Aunts

My Family

Thessaly Catt

PowerKiDS press™

New York

Published in 2011 by The Rosen Publishing Group, Inc.
29 East 21st Street, New York, NY 10010

First Edition

Editor: Maggie Murphy
Book Design: Ashley Burrell
Photo Researcher: Jessica Gerweck

Photo Credits: Cover Somos/Veer/Getty Images; p. 5 Siri Stafford/Getty Images; p. 7 (grandfather) © www.iStockphoto.com/Juanmonino; p. 7 (grandmother) © www.iStockphoto.com/Elena Ray; pp. 7 (mom, dad, aunt), 12–13 Shutterstock.com; p. 7 (sister) © www.iStockphoto.com/quavondo; p. 7 (brother) © www.iStockphoto.com/Ekaterina Monakhova; p. 7 (uncle) © www.iStockphoto.com/asiseeit; p. 7 (cousin) © www.iStockphoto.com/Aldo Murillo; pp. 8–9, 15, 16 Ariel Skelley/Getty Images; p. 10 Michael Poehlman/Getty Images; pp. 18–19, 20–21 Jupiterimages/Getty Images; p. 23 Paul Costello/Getty Images.

Library of Congress Cataloging-in-Publication Data

Catt, Thessaly.
  My uncles and aunts / Thessaly Catt. — 1st ed.
      p. cm. — (My family)
  Includes index.
  ISBN 978-1-4488-1464-0 (library binding) — ISBN 978-1-4488-1494-7 (pbk.) — ISBN 978-1-4488-1495-4 (6-pack)
  1. Aunts—Juvenile literature. 2. Uncles—Juvenile literature. I. Title.
  HQ759.94.C38 2011
  306.87—dc22

                                    2010008869

Manufactured in the United States of America
CPSIA Compliance Information: Batch #WS10PK: For Further Information contact Rosen Publishing, New York, New York at 1-800-237-9932

Contents

Many people have aunts and uncles. How many do you have?

Can you find the aunt and uncle on this **family tree**?

Family Tree

Grandfather

Grandmother

Uncle

Aunt

Dad

Mom

Cousin

Brother

Sister

Your aunts' and uncles' children are your **cousins**.

6

Rico visits his aunt Tina in New York. Where do your aunts and uncles live?

Juan and Sara play games with their uncle Marco and aunt Rosa.

What do you like to do with your aunts and uncles?

Every family is different. Nina lives with her aunt, uncle, and cousin.

Nick's family gets together at **Christmas**. When do you see your aunts and uncles?

Maria's aunts teach her how to make **tamales**. They are a favorite food in their family!

Your aunts and uncles are part of your family. They love you!

Words to Know

Christmas (KRIS-mus) A holiday that celebrates the birth of Christ.

cousins (KUH-zunz) The children of your aunts and uncles.

family tree (FAM-lee TREE) A chart that shows the members of a family.

tamales (tuh-MAH-leez) Mexican dishes made of corn that are stuffed with certain things.

Index

Web Sites

Due to the changing nature of Internet links, PowerKids Press has developed an online list of Web sites related to the subject of this book. This site is updated regularly. Please use this link to access the list: www.powerkidslinks.com/family/auntunc/